W9-BQK-056

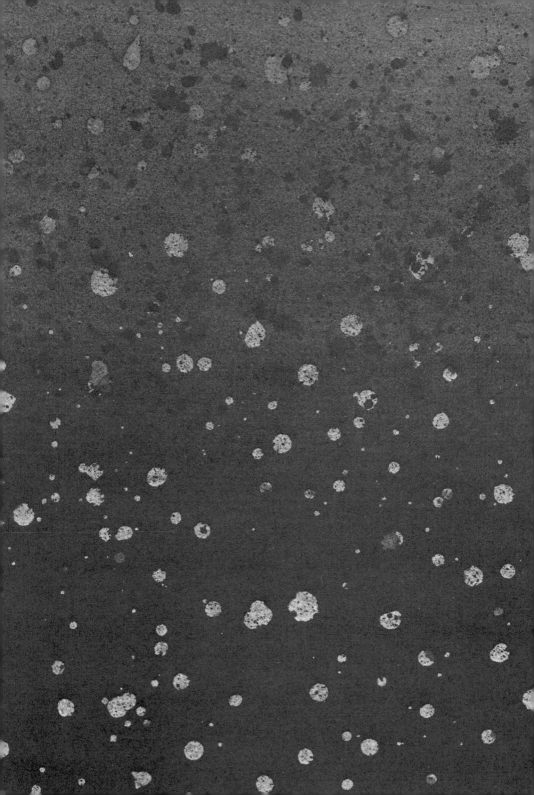

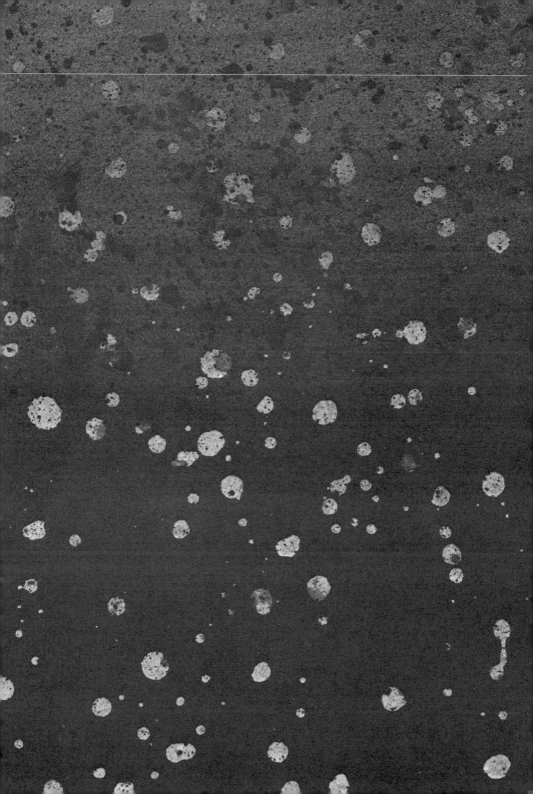

All the Colors of the Race

All the Colors of the Race

Poems by Arnold Adoff
Illustrated by John Steptoe

Beech Tree Books

CURR
PZ
7
.A274
A1
1992

FRANKLIN PIERCE
COLLEGE LIBRARY
RINDGE, N.H. 03461

All the colors of the race

All the colors of the race
are
       in my face, and just behind my face:
                behind my eyes:
       inside my head.

And inside my head, I give my self a place
       at the end of a long
                line   forming
                      it self into a
                        circle.

And I am holding out my hands.

I think the real color   is behind the color

I think the real color   is behind the color.
That
skin on
     my face   is for the cold mornings,
     and
     the cool breezes of some
                         summer afternoons.

Under that skin   and under that
                              face
              is the real
                   race.

Past

I have all these parts   stuffed in
                                                    me
like mama's chicken
                            and
                biscuits,
                            and
daddy's apple pie, and a tasty
                                        story
from the family
                    tree.

But I know that tomorrow
                            morning
            I'll wake up
                    empty, and hungry for that
                                                    next
                                                    bite
            of my new
                    day.

Great Grandma Ida

Great Grandma Ida came from a small village
in Poland
        on the Russian border.
        And her parents came
                    from that same village.
And their parents before them.

And sometime, long before that,
               these
people came from Spain.
        And a long
           time before that,
              those
people had come from places
               in the Middle
                  East
               or Africa,
across the Mediterranean Sea.

Borders

Great Grandma Ida came from a small village
in Poland
        on the Russian border
        to America,
        on a ship that   sailed
        for weeks,
        on the rough Atlantic
                        Ocean:

to make a new place for her self;
to work in a factory; to find her father;
to find a man
        from a German town on the Polish
                                border
to marry; to have and raise a daughter
        who would find and marry
        a man from a Russian town
                        on the Polish
                        border.

And in 1935 they would have a baby boy
        in a New York City hospital
who is daddy now to
        me.

I know we can go back so far

We can go back so far
so far
but only so far
and
not as far as forward.

One Great Grandma's family   was lost to us,
when they were marched to the Nazi death
camps
and their Polish town destroyed.

One Great Grandma's family was lost to us
in the years of slavery,
and in the Civil War
smoke of burning plantations.

I am making a circle for my self

I am making a circle for my self
                              and
I am placing into that
            circle: all who are for me,
                  and
                  all   that is inside.

If I am only   white and Jewish   then mama stays
                                          outside.
If I am only   black and Protestant
                              then daddy stays
                                    outside.

But Golda is in the circle. Ben Gurion. Moses.
And Grandpa Jack is
                  surely
            in.

I am making a circle for my self
                          and
I am placing into
          that circle: all who are for me;
                    all that is inside
                                        me.

If I am only black and Protestant:
          then daddy stays outside.
If I am only white and Jewish:
          then mama stays outside.

But Harriet is in the circle. Martin King. Malcolm.
And Great
     Grandpa Perry is
                    surely
                    in.

Still finding out

     Finding out that Grandpa Perry
was
born a slave   and died a free
               farmer
here in Ohio:
         I am
          free
here in Ohio
        on the Perry land: planting tomatoes
               on his same land.

I am part Perry
        and
    part still
        finding
         out.

I am

Mama is black
          and
          daddy
          is white
and
I am black
and
I am white:

          besides
my age
     and
     sex
     and
        clarinet.

Flavors

Mama is chocolate: you must be swirls
                         of dark fudge,
                    and ripples
                              through
                    your cocoa
                         curls;
chips
      and
flips of sprinkles
      on your
           summer
           face.

18

Flavors

Daddy is vanilla: you must be mean
                                  old
                               bean
                    in the morning,
                    cherry
                    chunks by afternoon,
                    and
                        sweet
                        peach sometimes.

But mostly   you
             are vanilla
                      up
                 your
                 arms.

Flavors

Me
is better
   butter: I must be
              pecans
                    roasted,
                    toasted;
almond
wal nut   three
         scoop combination
                cone:
melting under
     kisses.

It is a new color.
It is a new flavor.
     For
       love.

On my applications

On my applications   I can
                            put:
this girl:
        a black,
            white,
Christian,
Jewish,
        young
        woman:
            student,
            musician,
singer,
dancer,
runner   in the middle distance races,

        is willing to help you
        if you take her as she
                            is.

Trilingual

I can talk
         black,
  and
I can talk
         white,
  and
I can talk
        so no
         one
understands.

Four
Foot
Feat

Imagine I am standing with
                    one
                    foot
in Africa: for my
                    ancestors
dragged away from their
homes and lands and tribes
to sail to
          America as
                    slaves.

                    One
                    foot
in Europe: for my
                    ancestors
living in their ghettos, in
their Polish and German
villages, until they
                    sailed
to America to find
a new home and
               life.

Imagine I am standing with
one
foot
in New York City: for my
first eight years of
riding
the Central Park carousel;
walking on Broadway;
listening
to the music
of the streets.

One
foot
in Ohio: for my present
time of summer corn
and the smell of hogs
after rain.
This
town
has birds that bring
the mornings to my
room.

Four foot feat: enough to make me sit
right down.

The lady said:

The lady said: what are you going to
                                          be
                    when you grow
                    all the way up?

And I said: a woman.

And she said.   No. I mean what are
                                        you
                                        now?
And I said: a girl.

And she said: No. I mean what do you call
                                            yourself?
And I said: Honey. Baby. Sweet
                          potato
                          pie
                                face me.

If she finds it hard,
            I find it easy
        to make it hard for her.

I know the rules

I know the rules   and I am what I am
                                    because
                    I can say
                            what I am,
                    and what I need,
                    and what I hope to become
                                    in this world.
That is the rule I add for me.

My eyes can see
            and lips smile
            and lips kiss.

Arms can stretch out
                    and
            circle:
                    hold
                    and
                    hug.

There is so much

There is so much
in the way we all live
that
         separates: it must be hard
                      for some people
to see
daddy reaching   over
                    me
to kiss
mama in the grocery,
or see
mama laugh
        and hug
                daddy
        in the street.

Bad guys

We live the same: our way,
and walk
       the same;
and talk,
       no matter where we live
          and go.
And most people
smile at us   on sunny Ohio afternoons
       in parks and restaurants.
But
while we talk and smile
and eat
    our way through
       Sundays, we keep a corner
         of our eyes   for
           any

      bad guys.

Some old ones

Some old ones   talk about:
                          this one
                is
                so dark,
and
     that
one   is
        so light,   and
                           this
                one
has such
     hair.

But the young ones
                  talk about:
                          brothers
                               and
                          sisters.

Passing

            they called it
                        in the old days:
supposed to
            be millions
                        crossed that magic
                                    line:
to live as white;
to give up the daily struggle
    for good:
    give up grandmas   and the   land.

Can we wipe it with our lives?
Can we wipe it the way you
            wipe a chalk line
            with your
                        hand?
Or is
    it running up my spine?

I   was   Harriet

I   was   Harriet
in
    the   play

    and
          got
    to   lead
          them
    all
          to
          free
    dom.

At the meeting

At the meeting
            they said they wanted to send
one white
        and one black kid to the celebration,
to make it even and equal.
So
I said to just send me   and it would still be
                                    fair,
and we could still
            save one round-trip fare.

Then they waited to see if I was smiling
before they laughed,
and my motion lost because I forgot
            I couldn't be a boy.

We are talking about

We are talking about
                    the ones who pick   their friends
                    because of how   black   they act
                                                          or
                    because of how   white   they can
                                                         be.

Sometimes blackness seems too black for me,
            and whiteness is too   sickly pale;
            and I wish every
                        one were golden from
                                            the
                                    sun.
            Golden from the
                            inside
            out.

In our one family

In our one family, around
                    this
            round
            table
of our nights and days:
                    we are together
                    in old ways,
                    we are together
                    in new ways.

Pancakes and chicken. Pork chops and cream:
        we
        are new people
                eating our way
to a new time
            of
        love.
                We are trying for the
                            dream.

When they asked

When they asked
if
I was black or white
            or what,
I said:
I was black and
                white
            and what
difference
did it make to them.

And they said:
did I have the answers
                        to the math
                        problems?
And
I had the answers.

Sum People

The   black   man
                  said
I was a   half
                  breed,
but I told
                  him
to
check   out   his
                  math:
like
        one
                  plus
        one.

A song:

      I have the fore
              head
      of the black
              Ohio
      farmers
      looking
at the
   sky
   for rain.

      Baby
      Blue.

And my nose
has   that Russian
             Jewish
      bump.

      Jump.

I can do my hair

I can do my hair   short
                            and
                    curled
                        tight
on my head,
or let it
        grow
        long, and wave it
                like the
                        rest
        of my friends.

I look in the mirror
and see
    me standing with a brush.
I have just arrived.
I am in a rush. I want to be
                            the
                        best.

If they hate me

If they hate me
   they
are
   sick
and
   hurt
and
   need
   some
   kind
of
   help.

I will
   stay
right
   here.

For every one

For every one   we know the inside
                              blood
                              is
                                   blue:
and when we cut,
            or scrape,
            or scratch
                        below the skin
the outside blood
                   is red:
                   is red for every
                              one.

True: red for every one.

A song:

I am of the earth   and the earth is of me.
I am all the colors of the corn field,
                and the corn field
    is all the colors of me.
I am all the colors of the plowed-up garden,
                and the plowed-up garden
    is all the colors of me.
I am of the earth   and the earth is of me.

We are together   under the blue sky.
We are together   under the yellow
                                sun.
We are together   under the gray
                                clouds.
We are together:
                sisters.

In both the families

In both the families
that
   both belong to me,
there is every shade
of
brown, and tan,
and paler
      honey,
creamy gold.

I face faces that I see
in
   both the families
that
   both belong to me,
and
they can face
my crooked
    grin.

Here is every shade of every color
              skin.
   We fit in.

The way I see any hope for later

The way I see any hope for later,
we will have to get
                over this color
                        thing,
and stop looking
                at how much brown
                or tan there is
                                in
                or on   this
                        woman
                or that   man.
And stop looking
                at who is a woman
                and
                who is a man.

Stop looking.
Start loving.

Remember:

Remember: long ago   before people moved
                       and migrated, and mixed and
                                           matched
                   their arms
side
      by
side
      in European caves;

      or captured slaves
were
sent in ships around this earth;

                  long ago   there was one people:
                              one color,
                              one race.

Of the race

Some day   I will have babies with
high
foreheads   and curled
hair,
and darker places,
browner eyes.

The colors are flowing
from
what was before
me
to what will
be
after.

All the colors.

All the colors of the race

All the colors of the race. Human, of course.
   Beginning in Africa, in Asia, in the
                        Middle
                        East,
   and long before Plymouth
                Rock.

In ancient kingdoms the people are firing
            clay heads for their gods;
                  mixing
        colors
        for the headcloths
        of the mothers.

Mixing   colors.
Mixing
      colors.

All the colors of the race. Human, of course.

Dedication:

For my children, Jaime and Leigh, and for their
brothers and sisters of every race
and every
wonderful combination of races.

Direction:

This book is a presentation of power and love.
Celebrate the meaning and music
of your lives.
Stand free and take control.

Text copyright © 1982 by Arnold Adoff. Illustrations copyright © 1982 by John Steptoe.
All rights reserved. No part of this book may be reproduced or utilized in any form or by
any means, electronic or mechanical, including photocopying, recording or by any
information storage and retrieval system, without permission in writing from the
Publisher. Inquiries should be addressed to Lothrop, Lee & Shepard Books, a division
of William Morrow & Company, Inc., 1350 Avenue of the Americas, New York,
NY 10019. Printed in the United States of America. First Beech Tree Edition, 1992.
1 2 3 4 5 6 7 8 9 10

Library of Congress Cataloging-in-Publication Data.   Adoff, Arnold.   All the colors of
the race.   Summary: A collection of poems written from the point of view of a child
with a black mother and a white father.   1. Children's poetry, American.   2. Family—
Juvenile poetry.   3. Race awareness—Juvenile poetry.   [1. American poetry.
2. Family—Poetry.   3. Race awareness—Poetry]   I. Steptoe, John, (date), ill.
II. Title.
PS3551.D66A77   811'.54   81-11777
ISBN 0-688-11496-2

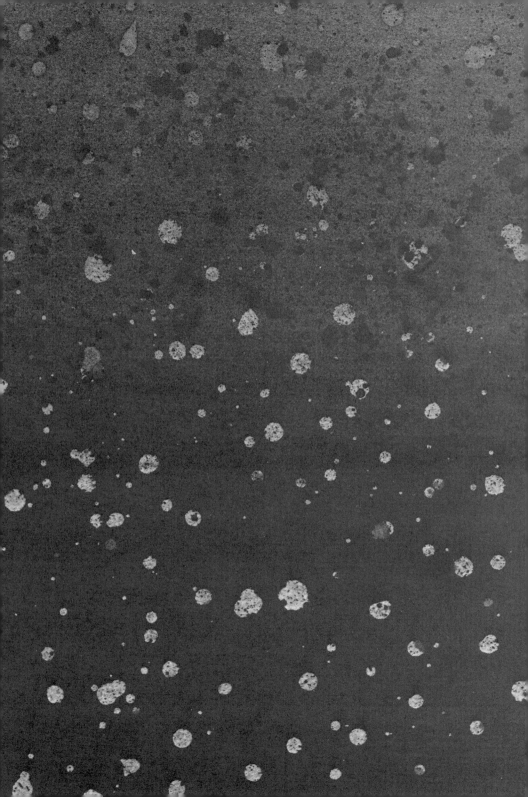